The Co
Cookbook

Over 30 Delicious Coffee Recipes

Thomas Kelly

INTRODUCTION

Coffee is one of the best and tastiest drinks that you can enjoy today. There are many different coffee drinks that are available today, but even with these numerous options most people tend to stick to the same type of coffee each and every time. However, whenever you explore new varieties of coffee you will begin to find new favorite types of coffee that you may fall in love with.

We all know how it is to have that first cup of coffee in the morning. There is nothing better than it. What if I told you that there were different coffee flavors out there when you use them, they tend to dim the brightness of the coffee while enhancing the overall flavor of it. Well there are many different coffee flavors out there that you can try and find what kind of flavors you like the most.

In this book you will be able to find the different coffee flavors that will surely get your taste buds going. This books is packed full of tasty coffee recipes that you are going to drool over.

So, let's not waste any more time. Let's start brewing!

TABLE OF CONTENTS

Chapter One: The Common Myths about Drinking Coffee

Coffee happens to be one of the most popular drinks in the entire world. This kind of drink has become extremely important for many of us, especially during the morning as it helps us to stay awake when we know there is just too much to do throughout the day. There are so many different types of coffee out there that sometimes it can be hard to choose the perfect one.

However, just as there are that many types of coffee, there are just that many myths about it. There are many myths out there that claim coffee in general is bad for you, when research and scientific studies may say otherwise. The truth of the matter is that coffee can be very beneficial for you, though you may not be aware of it. In this chapter you will discover some of the most popular myths out there about coffee and why they are that: myths.

Myth #1: Coffee Can Make You Feel Stressed

The myth that coffee can make you feel stressed out is very humorous. Since caffeine itself is known as a stimulate and a positive one at that, coffee is in no responsible for triggering stress in the first place.

Myth #2: Caffeine Can Cause Insomnia

This is perhaps one of the most common myths about coffee or any other kind of drink that contains caffeine. This myth is simply not true. What happens every time you drink a cup of coffee is that your body instantly absorbs it, but then gets rid of it just as quickly. As soon as it is consumed the caffeine will go through your liver where about 50% of it will be flushed out of your body within 4 to 5 hours. After 5 hours almost 75% of that caffeine will be shed out of your body entirely. You should be suffering from sleeping problems just because you are drinking coffee, as long as you drink no more than 2 to 3 cups of coffee a day.

Myth #3: Drinking Coffee Can Cause Cancer

There is yet another myth often associated with drinking coffee or caffeinated products and that is that they will eventually cause cancer. This is simply not true and there are many scientific studies to back up these findings. There have been studies conducted on this subject matter and all of them have found that there is no direct correlation between drinking coffee and the formation of cancer.

In fact there are many studies that have been conducted and that have found those who drink coffee on a daily basis were actually able to reduce the risk of them developing cancer in the future. Coffee itself is packed full of healthy antioxidants that can help you fight cancer and it also help to reduce the effects of aging, making you look younger than you actually are.

Myth #4: Coffee Contains No Health Benefits

As you will learn in the next chapter, this is a myth that it is simply not true. Coffee not only contains helpful antioxidants, but it has also been proved that coffee can improve your heart function and can prevent the formation of cancer. We'll go into the actual benefits of drinking coffee in the next chapter.

Myth #5: Caffeine Can Be Extremely Addictive

There are many people who drink coffee on a daily basis feel compelled to claim that they are addicted to caffeine simply because they feel as if they cannot live with it. The definition of addiction is severely depending on a drug and experiencing withdrawal symptoms when you do not get that specific drug in a certain amount. Consuming caffeine is not actually classified as an addiction by scientific research and there have been many studies conducted that found caffeine is not able to form any kind of addiction.

Other substances such as alcohol or any other kind of drug can cause not only severe social consequences, but it can cause physical consequences as well and this is not the case with caffeine.

Myth #6: Drinking Coffee Can Cause Miscarriage, Low Birth Weight and Infertility in Women

This is yet another popular misconception about coffee and there is no strong evidence to prove that it is true. In fact scientists have found that there is no link correlated between coffee and the chance of miscarriages. There are many women out there who have drank coffee on a regular basis while they are pregnant and yet have babies that are born at normal weight, myself included. Similarly there are women out there who drink coffee on a day-to-day basis and have no problem getting problem. So, in the end this myth is completely untrue.

Myth #7: Coffee Can Cause Osteoporosis

This is another common myth about coffee that has no facts or research to back it up. The only way that you can suffer from osteoporosis is either by developing it due to family history, or by not consuming enough Vitamin D or calcium in your everyday diet. There are many other factors that can contribute to the development of osteoporosis such as menopause, low estrogen levels and active smoking. There have been no studies ever conducted that have found that caffeine can contribute to the development of this condition at all.

Chapter Two: The Benefits of Coffee

You would be surprised at how healthy coffee can actually be for you. Not only is one cup loaded full of powerful antioxidants, but there are many beneficial nutrients that have been proven to enhance your overall health as well. In this chapter you will find 13 benefits of coffee that are all backed up by evidence to prove them.

1. Drinking Coffee Can Help Improve Your Energy Levels and Enhance Your Brain Power

Coffee is the perfect drink to indulge in especially if you are feeling tired. Drinking coffee will help you to feel less tired and will actually increase the amount of energy that you have. Why is this? It is because there is a known stimulant that can be found in coffee and the moment you drink a cup it immediately travels through your bloodstream, and right into your brain.

Once in your brain the caffeine will work to block a component known as Adenosine. Once that occurs the levels of norepinephrine and dopamine actually increase, firing hundreds of neurons almost simultaneously.

There have been many studies conducted on this and found that when people drink coffee they were able to show increase memory, higher energy levels, faster reaction time and enhance cognitive function.

2. Coffee Can Help You to Lose Weight

Have you ever noticed that the moment you have a cup of coffee, you are suddenly not as tired as you were before? That is because caffeine, a known substance found in coffee, is found in many fat burning supplements used today and there is actual fact and studies that back this up. Caffeine happens to be one of the very few substances on the planet today that have been proven to help in weight loss.

The many studies that have been conducted on this subject have shown that caffeine can help boost the average metabolic rate by at least 3 to

11%. These studies have also show that caffeine can actually help to burn fat by as much as 10% in people who are considered overweight and by as much as 29% in people who are considered to be lean.

3. Caffeine Can Help Enhance Your Overall Physical Appearance

Caffeine is one substance that has been proven to stimulate the entire nervous system, causing it to send specific signals to the brain that will tell cells to begin burning fat within the body. However, caffeine is also known to be able to increase Epinephrine levels within the blood, giving your body the energy boost that it may need. This hormone is popularly known as the "fight or flight" response and it prepares your body to brace itself for some kind of physical exertion that is about to take place.

Given this particular effect, many studies have found that caffeine can help to improve a person's physical performance by at least 11-12%. Knowing these facts it makes perfect sense to have at least 1 strong cup of coffee right before you are about to work out. It will help improve your workout and give you the energy that you need to complete it.

4. Can Help You Get Essential Nutrients That You Need

I know that when you look at coffee it can look like nothing but black colored water. However, it is packed full of important nutrients that your body needs and most of these nutrients can be found in the black beans of your coffee.

Some of the nutrients that black coffee beans include are:

1. Riboflavin or Vitamin B
2. Pantothenic Acid of Vitamin B5
3. Manganese

4. Potassium
5. Niacin

Although while some of these nutrients may not seem as if they are a big deal, they are important for a variety of different functions within your body. If you drink more than once cup of coffee each and every day, the amount of each nutrient that you can consume will quickly add up and benefit your body in a variety of different ways.

5. Coffee Can Help Lower Your Risk of Developing Type 2 Diabetes

Type 2 Diabetes is one health epidemic that affects more than 300 million different people around the globe. This illness is often characterized by many different symptoms such as high blood sugar levels and irritability. For people who drink coffee on a daily basis, they are able to decrease the risk of developing this disease in the future.

There have been many studies conducted and that have found that people who drink the most coffee are less likely to develop this condition by as much as 23 to 50% percent. When you look at it, this is a significant number.

6. Coffee Can Help Reduce the Risk of Alzheimer's and Dementia

Alzheimer's is one of the most common mental disease that affects many seniors worldwide and it is the primary cause of dementia as the person gets older. Unfortunately there is no cure for Alzheimer's as of today, but scientist are quickly trying to find one and should be able to find one in the future.

There are many things that you can do right now to help prevent the development of this disease such as eating a healthy and well balanced diet. However, one of the best ways to prevent this disease is to drink coffee on a daily basis. There have been many studies conducted that found drinking coffee on a daily basis can prevent the development of this disease by at least 65%.

7. Caffeine Can Help To Lower the Development of Parkinson's

Parkinson's is yet another brain degenerative disease following Alzheimer's. This disease is often caused by neurons in the brain responsible for developing a hormone known as dopamine completely dying off. Similar to Alzheimer's, there is no known cure for this disease, but there are many different ways that you can prevent it from developing altogether. One of those ways is by drinking plenty of coffee.

It has been found that people who drink coffee on a daily basis are able to reduce the risk of developing this disease by up to 32 to 60% then those who do not drink caffeine.

8. Caffeine Can Help To Protect Your Liver

This liver, while an amazing organ in itself, is extremely important. This organ is responsible for carry out a variety of different function within the body. Just as there are many functions of the liver, there are just as many disease that can plague it such as fatty liver disease and hepatitis. Some of the disease that can plague the liver can also cause a condition known as cirrhosis, in which the entire liver is covered in a layer of scar tissue.

Coffee is an excellent way to protect the liver from this particular condition. In studies performed it was found that many people who drink 4 or more cups of coffee every day are able to lower their risk of developing this condition by as much as 80%.

9. Caffeine Can Help Ward Off Depression

Depression is a very serious mental disorder and it is one that should be taken seriously. When people suffer from depression it can significantly reduce the quality of life that a person has and can literally make one's life a living hell.

In a study recently conduct by Harvard in 2011, it found that women who drank more than 4 cups of coffee on a daily basis had a reduced risk of developing depression by at least 20%. In another study that was conducted, it was found that avid coffee drinkers were less likely to commit suicide by as much as 53%.

10. Caffeine Can Help Reduce the Risk of Developing Cancer

Cancer is single most leading cause of death in the world today. It is often characterized by cells growing uncontrollable within the body and that are malignant. By drinking coffee on a daily basis, you can prevent two types of cancer: Colon cancer and liver cancer. Liver cancer is the third most lethal type of cancer today, followed by colon cancer.

There have been many different kinds of studies conducted and that found people who drank coffee on a regular basis were able to lower the risk of developing liver cancer by up to 40%. There was even another studied conducted that found people who drank more than 4 to 5 cups of coffee every day were able to reduce the risk of developing colon cancer by as much as 15%.

11. Coffee Can Reduce The Chance of Developing Heart Disease and Stroke

There are many people out there that claim caffeine often increase one's blood pressure to dangers levels. While this is slightly true, the truth is that caffeine will not raise the blood pressure that high. It will only raise it by 3 to 4 small hit and will usually go away if you drink coffee on a regular basis. However, if you are suffering from high blood pressure, keep in mind that caffeine can raise your blood pressure slightly.

With that being said, there are no studies that can prove that drinking coffee will lead to heart disease. Contrary to popular belief there is evidence that show women who drink coffee on a regular basis can reduce the risk of developing heart disease. Also these studies have been able to show that people who drink coffee can reduce their risk of stroke by up to 20%.

12. Caffeine Can Help You Live Much Longer

While so far we have shown that people who drink coffee are able to reduce the risk of developing some popular disease out there, this benefit should be no surprise. It just makes sense that drinking plenty of coffee will help you to live a healthier and much longer life. To back this claim up there have been many studies conducted that found people who drink coffee on a regular basis are able to decrease their risk of death significantly.

In two recent studies, it was found that people who drank coffee regularly were able to reduce their risk of death by up to 20% in men and 26% in women throughout the world. This study was conducted on people within the age of 18 to 24 years.

However, this effect was primarily strong in individuals who had type 2 diabetes. In one study it was found that diabetics who regularly drank coffee were able to reduce the risk of death by as much as 30% during a span of 20 years.

13. Coffee Happens To Be the Largest Source of Antioxidants Today

For people who consume a regular Western diet on a daily basis, the healthiest aspect of that entire diet may be the cup of coffee you have on a daily basis. Why is this? It is because coffee is known for having the most antioxidants out of any other drink that you can have today. To back this up there have been many studies conducted that found that people are able to get more antioxidants out of drinking coffee on a regular basis than they would by consuming whole fruits and vegetables.

The bottom line that was outlined in this chapter is one undisputable fact: coffee is one of the healthiest drinks that you can drink…period. If you are looking for a drink that you can enjoy on a daily basis and that you can strongly benefit from, it is coffee.

Chapter Three: Five Essential Tools That You Need To Make The Perfect Cup of Coffee Every Time

Some of the fun in making your own homebrewed coffee is the entire process or trying to make a perfect cup of coffee. Making a perfect cup of coffee is not going to happen all on its own. It is going to require you to have the right tools on hand in order to achieve it. There are many different tools that you can use to make your perfect coffee and we will explore those tools in depth in this chapter.

There are essential tools that you are going to need in order to make: The tools that you should have on hand:

1. A coffee grinding tool.
2. A tool to boil some water in.
3. A tool to make your coffee in
4. A coffee mug

There are various tools out there that you can invest it. Depending on what you budget is and what you are looking for specifically.

1. A Manual Brewing System

If you have yet to try your hand at hand brewing, it is something that you really have to do. Now is the perfect time to give it a go and I know for a fact that you will not regret it. There are many different manual brewing systems out there and the one that will work best for you will ultimately depend on what you like. I always recommend that you start with the simplest manual brewing system and then upgrade once you have gotten the hang of it.

Keep in mind, there are a variety of brewing systems out there so collect as many systems at you can so you can find one that is perfect for you.

2. A Digital Scale

While I know that weighing your coffee may seem like an odd thing to do, it is actually important. You will need to make sure that your bean to water ratio is as perfect as possible since it will affect the overall taste of your coffee. Now, don't use a bathroom scale. You really need to invest in a good kitchen scale in order to do the job correctly.

You will need to make sure that you use a kitchen scale that not only measures weight, but that also measures time and flow rates as well.

3. A Burr Grinder

The best thing about this grinder is how versatile it is. It is usually small in size so you can take it with you wherever you may end up. Of course this is a product that you will need to invest in if you do not mind putting a little work into making your coffee in the morning.

4. A Traditional Water Kettle

There are many people today that have a standard electric kettle probably sitting in their kitchen. However, if you do not have one yet, it is time that you look into purchasing one. You can choose from a variety of different kettles such as one that you may find in traditional coffee shops or one that is able to control its temperature. However, feel free to invest into whatever type of kettle may work best for you.

5. A Drip Brew System

If you are really committed into making the perfect cup of coffee each and every time, then you simply cannot go wrong in investing in more elaborate coffee making systems such as a drip and cold brew system. There are many to choose out there so feel free to splurge out on whatever system you can afford.

Rules to Making Perfect Coffee

Now that you have the tools and equipment that you need in order to make coffee, it is time to teach you about the rules in order to do so. Specifically there are 9 rules that you have to follow in order to achieve this and by following these rules you will soon become a coffee brewing master yourself.

Rule #1: Always Buy Fresh Coffee Beans

There is no question that the best time to make coffee is when you are using beans days before you are actually roasting them. I recommend purchasing beans from a local coffee bean roaster (if you can find one). I would be cautious around coffee beans that are displayed at the supermarket for a few reasons. One, the oxygen and bright light that are exposed to the beans tend to ruin the flavor of them so they will not taste as good as fresh beans. Two, most of the beans have already gone rancid.

You are much better off buying coffee beans that are in vacuum sealed bags and are packed by high quality and professional roasters.

Rule #2: Always Keep Your Coffee Beans Fresh

Once you have your coffee beans on hand, always make sure to lock them in an airtight container immediately. Never place your beans into your refrigerator and the beans can become moist and quickly go bad. For best results always buy no more than a 5 to 7 day supply of beans and try to keep them at room temperature.

Rule #3: Grind Your Own Beans

The moment that you grind up coffee beans, the faster they will begin to lose their quality. For the highest quality and best tasting coffee always grind up your beans the moment you are about to make coffee. Trust me, you will immediately notice the difference in taste the moment you take a sip.

Rule #4: Use a High Quality Water Source

I know that most of us are used to using simple tap water in order to make our coffee and the truth is that will only ruin the flavor. The best type of water that you can use to make coffee is bottle water or filtered water. The water will contain all of the nutrients that natural coffee has to offer and it will help to give the coffee a more improved taste.

Rule #5: Never Use Cheap Filters

If there is one thing that you should always invest your money on, it is durable coffee filters. There have been many studies that have shown cheap priced coffee filters tend to yield in most undesirable coffees. I highly recommend investing in a gold plated filter as they help to deliver maximum taste to every cup of coffee that you make and will last a long time.

Rule #6: Never Skimp On Your Coffee

This rule is important to follow as using the correct ratio can yield the tastiest coffee. The exact measurement that you have to follow is 2 Tablespoons of coffee per every 6 ounce cup of water that is used. If you use less coffee than recommend, I promise you that you will only end up with a bitter and nasty tasting brew.

Alpine Carnival Coffee

This coffee will make you feel as if you are right there in the French Alps. This coffee is incredibly smooth, but strong, giving you the energy boost that you deserve in the morning.

Makes:	1 ½ Cup of Coffee
Total Prep Time:	10 Minutes

INGREDIENTS:

- 2 Tbsp. of Instant Coffee
- 1 tsp. of Vanilla
- 2 Tbsp. of Brown Sugar, Packed and Light
- 1 tsp. of Water
- 1 ½ Cup of Water, Boiling
- ½ Cup of Whipping Cream, Fully Whipped

DIRECTIONS:

1. The first thing that you will want to do is divide up your coffee and your vanilla. Divide them between two Spanish style coffee glasses.
2. Then using a small sized saucepan dissolve your sugar with at least 1 teaspoon of water. Warm over medium heat and continuously stir until your sugar water reaches a boil. Once boiling remove your mixture from heat and continue to stir.
3. Evenly divide up your sugar water between two different coffee glasses and finally top with a heaping dollop of whipping cream. Enjoy!

Classic Amaretto Style Coffee

If your favorite coffee is Amaretto, then you are going to drool over this recipe. Now you can make you favorite kind of coffee from the comfort of your own home without any of the hassle.

Makes: 2 Cups

Total Prep Time: 10 Minutes

INGREDIENTS:

- 1 ½ Cup of Water, Warm
- 1/3 Cup of Amaretto
- 1 Tbsp. of Instant Coffee, Crystals
- Dessert Topping, From A Can

DIRECTIONS:

1. Using a measure cup, stir together your warm water and instant coffee together until fully dissolved.
2. Then place into a microwave uncovered and microwave for at least 4 minutes or until your mixture is steaming hot.
3. Last, stir in your Amaretto until fully dissolves. Serve in your favorite coffee mugs and top with your dessert topping. Enjoy.

Arabian Style Coffee

Now, this is a type of coffee that you find in many coffee shops today as one of the most basic blends offered. This is a strong and robust coffee, making a great cup of coffee each and every time.

Makes: 1 Pint of Coffee

Total Prep Time: 5 Minutes

INGREDIENTS:

- 1 Pint of Water
- 3 Tbsp. of Coffee, Your Favorite Kind
- 3 Tbsp. of Sugar, Maybe More
- ¼ tsp. of Cinnamon
- ¼ tsp. of Cardamom
- 1 tsp. of Vanilla

DIRECTIONS:

1. Mix all of your ingredients together in a medium sized saucepan. Place over medium heat and continue to stir until foam begins to gather at the top.
2. Remove from heat but do not pass the mixture through a filter. Continue stirring and then serve immediately.

BLACK FOREST COFFEE

This coffee is especially strong, making it the perfect choice for those looking for an added kick in their morning brew.

Makes:	6 Ounces of Coffee
Total Prep Time:	10 Minutes

INGREDIENTS:

- 6 Ounces of Brewed Coffee, Fresh
- 2 Tbsp. of Chocolate Syrup
- 1 Tbsp. of Cherry Juice, Maraschino Variety
- Some Whipped Cream, For Topping
- Some Chocolate Chips, Shaved or Solo
- Some Cherries, Maraschino Variety

DIRECTIONS:

1. The first thing that you will want to do is combine your chocolate syrup, cherry juice and coffee together in a cup. Mix together well until blended.
2. Once thoroughly mixed serve your coffee in a few cups and top with some whipped cream, a cherry and your chocolate shavings to make a decadent treat.

Italian Style Iced Coffee

If you are a big fan of iced coffee then you are going to fall in love with this recipe. This recipe has a classic Italian taste that you will love and that will leave you craving for more.

Makes: 4 ½ Cups of Coffee

Total Prep Time: 12 Hours and 5 Minutes

INGREDIENTS:

- 2 ½ Cups of Water, Cold
- 1 ½ Cups of Coffee, Ground and Seattle's Best Brand
- ¼ Cup of Coffee Mate, Fat Free and Italian Sweet Variety
- 1 to 2 tsp. of Splenda
- 1 tsp. of Cinnamon

DIRECTIONS:

1. Using a large sized mixing bowl, combine 1 cup of water that is cold and your coffee grounds together. Stir together with a spoon to gently combine all of your ingredients together. As you stir slowly add in your remaining cold water, being careful not to agitate your coffee grounds in the process.
2. Stop stirring and cover your bowl with a lid or some plastic wrap. Allow your grounds to steep at room temperature for at least 12 hours.
3. After this time strain your coffee through a coffee strainer and strain your contents into a pitcher.
4. Serve your coffee with at least 1 part of your coffee to 3 parts water and some ice cubes.

EASY COFFEE WITH MILK

If you are looking for an easy coffee recipe that will get you the cup o' joe that you need without any of the hassle, then you have to try this recipe out for yourself. It is incredibly easy to make and tastes delicious.

Makes: 3 Cups of Coffee

Total Prep Time: 5 Minutes

INGREDIENTS:

- 1 Cup of Milk
- 1 Cup of Cream, Light
- 3 Tbsp. of Coffee, Instant
- 2 Cups of Water, Boiling

DIRECTIONS:

1. Over low heat, heat up some milk and cream until your mixture is piping hot.
2. As your milk and cream are heating up, dissolve your coffee in some boil water.
3. Just before serving your coffee, make sure that you beat your milk mixture roughly and thoroughly with a beater until the mixture is frothy and foamy.
4. Then pour your milk mix into a warmed up pitcher and pour your coffee into another.
5. To serve your drink simply fill up a cup with both of your mixture simultaneously until the cup is filled. Enjoy!

Louisiana Style Coffee

Now this is a cup of coffee that will give you the kick you have been looking for. This cup of coffee contain chicory which gives this drink a bit of spice that every cup of coffee needs.

Makes: 3 Cups of Coffee

Total Prep Time: 5 Minutes

INGREDIENTS:

- 2 Cups of Milk, Whole
- Some Sugar, The Amount That You Desire
- 1 Cup of Coffee, Louisiana Style and With Chicory

DIRECTIONS:

1. Pour your whole milk into a small sized saucepan and heat over medium heat. Heat your mixture until it reaches a full boil.
2. Meanwhile brew your coffee in a coffee maker and add it into a cup while it is still piping hot. Pour in your milk at the same time. Sweeten with your desired amount of sugar to taste and enjoy immediately.

Traditional Café Au Cin

This coffee is very popular in many western countries as it is seen to have many medicinal properties. If you are looking for a cup of coffee that is packed full of a couple of healthy benefits, then this is the type of coffee recipe for you.

Makes: 2 ½ Cups of Coffee

Total Prep Time: 3 Minutes

INGREDIENTS:

- 1 Cup of Coffee, French Roast Variety, Cold and Strong Preferable
- 2 Tbsp. of Sugar, Granulated
- A Dash of Cinnamon, For Garnish and For Taste
- 2 Ounces of Tawny Port
- ½ tsp. of Orange Peel, Grated

DIRECTIONS:

1. The first thing that you will want to do is combine all of your ingredients together into a blender. Blend on the highest setting until completely smooth and creamy in consistency.
2. Pour your mixture into a few chilled glasses and enjoy.

Classic Café Style Cappuccino

A fresh brewed cup of cappuccino is one of the best ways to drink coffee today. This recipe will help you to make the perfect cappuccino each and every time and will leave your guests craving for more.

Makes:	2 Cups of Coffee
Total Prep Time:	5 Minutes

INGREDIENTS:

- ½ Cup of Coffee, Instant Variety
- ¾ Cup of Sugar, White
- 1 Cup of Milk, Non Fat and Dry

DIRECTIONS:

1. The first thing that you will want to do is use a mortar and pestle to crush your instant coffee into a fine powder. Then add in 2 tablespoons of coffee to each cup of hot water that you use.
2. Pour into cups. Then beat your milk with a beater until it is foamy.
3. Pour coffee into cups and tops with your foamed milk. Add as much sugar as you like and serve immediately.

Café Con Miel

This is a traditional Spanish style coffee that is particularly popular in Spain. It contains a robust flavor that you will surely fall in love with.

Makes: 4 Cups of Coffee

Total Prep Time: 10 Minutes

INGREDIENTS:

- 2 Cups of Coffee, Pre Made
- ½ Cup of Milk, Whole
- 4 Tbsp. of Honey, Feel Free To Add More If You Wish
- 1/8 tsp. of Cinnamon, Ground
- Dash of Nutmeg or Allspice, Optional
- Dash of Vanilla

DIRECTIONS:

1. Using a medium sized saucepan, heat up all of your ingredients together except for your nutmeg and allspice. Stir well until thoroughly combined.
2. Pour into cups and serve this as a light and tasty dessert. Enjoy!

Mexican Style Café De Ola

If you are looking for a traditional Spanish style coffee, it really does not get much better than this. This recipe is considered a favorite among many Mexican locals. However, it is extremely bold in flavor and strong so try not to drink this recipe after 5 pm unless you want to stay up all night.

Makes: 10 Cups of Coffee

Total Prep Time: 12 Minutes

INGREDIENTS:

- 8 Cups of Water
- 2 Cinnamon Sticks, Small In Size
- 3 Cloves, Whole
- 4 Ounces of Brown Sugar, Dark and Packed
- 1 Square of Chocolate, Mexican Style
- 4 Ounces of Coffee, Ground

DIRECTIONS:

1. The first thing that you will want to do is first bring your water to a rolling boil in a medium sized saucepan. Once boiling add in your whole cloves, cinnamon sticks, square of chocolate and sugar. Continuously stir until the chocolate is fully melted and your ingredients are evenly blended together.
2. If you notice any foam beginning to form, skim it off. Then reduce the heat to a low simmer. Make sure that you water does not continue to boil.
3. Next add in your ground coffee and allow it to steep for at least 5 minutes.
4. Serve your coffee in a pot and serve immediately.

Classic Café Alva Cocoa

If you are looking for a traditionally strong coffee, you need to try this recipe out for yourself. This coffee hails from the heart of Italy so you can rest assured that it is incredibly smooth, yet strong. This coffee will certainly give you the energy that you may need to survive the day.

Makes: 2 Cups of Coffee

Total Prep Time: 10 to 15 Minutes

INGREDIENTS:

- Some Amaretto Style Coffee Beans
- 1 Tbsp. of Vanilla Extract
- 1 tsp. of Almond Extract
- 1 tsp. of Cocoa Powder
- 1 tsp. of Sugar, White

DIRECTIONS:

1. Brew your coffee as you normally do every morning.
2. Pour your coffee into coffee mugs and serve with your added flavorings. Add at least 1 tsp. of chocolate and the desired amount of sugar.
3. Garnish your coffee with some whipped cream or sprinkles if you desire. Enjoy!

Déjà vu Vienna Coffee

This coffee recipe is given the name Déjà vu for a reason. This Vienna style coffee tastes and looks exactly the same as any other type of Vienna style coffee that you will try, but with a few subtle differences.

Makes: 2 Cups of Coffee

Total Prep Time: 5 Minutes

INGREDIENTS:

- ½ Cup of Coffee, Instant
- 2/3 Cup of Sugar, White
- 2/3 Cup of Milk, Nonfat and Dry
- ½ tsp. of Cinnamon, Ground
- Pinch of Cloves, Whole
- Pinch of Allspice
- Pinch of Nutmeg

DIRECTIONS:

1. Using a blender, blend up all of your ingredients together until it is a very fine powder. Then pour your coffee into your cups, making sure that you use at least 2 teaspoons per cup.
2. Pour your milk into your cups and serve with the desired amount of sugar. Serve and enjoy.

Orange Flavored Caffe Di Cioccolata

While I know orange flavored coffee may not sound appealing, don't knock this recipe before you try it. You may be surprised to find how tasty this kind of coffee really is.

Makes:	4 Cups of Water
Total Prep Time:	5 Minutes

INGREDIENTS:

- ¼ Cup of Espresso, Instant Variety
- ¼ Cup of Cocoa, Instant Variety
- 2 Cups of Water, Boiling
- Some Whipped Cream
- Orange Peel, Shredded Finely

DIRECTIONS:

1. The first thing that you will want to do is combine both your coffee and cocoa together. Then add in some boiling water and stir thoroughly until your mixture fully dissolves.
2. Pour your mixture into coffee cups and tops each cup with some whipped cream and finely shredded orange peel.

Orange Flavored Cappuccino

This is yet another orange flavored coffee drink that you simply have to try for yourself before passing judgment on it. This cappuccino is incredibly tasty, yet smooth when it goes down. I promise you will want to drink this drink over and over again.

Makes: 2 ½ Cups of Coffee

Total Prep Time: 5 Minutes

INGREDIENTS:

- ¼ Cup of Creamer, Non Dairy Preferable
- 1/3 Cup of Sugar, White
- ¼ Cup of Coffee, Instant and Dry Variety
- 1 or 2 Orange Candies, Hard and Dried

DIRECTIONS:

1. Using a large sized mixer, blend all of your ingredients together until thoroughly combines.
2. Then mix in at least 1 tablespoon of your mix with ¾ cup of steaming hot water. Serve this cup and store your leftover mix in an airtight jar. Serve as you desire and enjoy.

THE ULTIMATE CREAMY CAPPUCCINO

Who doesn't like a good cappuccino? Well, with this recipe you will be able to make the perfect cappuccino, and one that you will crave again and again.

Makes:	3 Cups of Coffee
Total Prep Time:	5 Minutes

INGREDIENTS:

- ¼ Cup of Espresso or Coffee, Instant or Dark Roast
- 2 Cups of Water, Boiling
- ½ Cup of Heavy Cream, Whipped
- Dash of Cinnamon or Nutmeg Option
- An Orange Peel, Shredded Finely

DIRECTIONS:

1. The first thing that you will want to do is dissolve your coffee or espresso in some boiling water.
2. Pour your coffee into small sized tall cups, making sure that you only fill it about half full.
3. Top with whipped cream and your optional toppings. Serve while still piping hot.

Tasty Cardamom Spicy Coffee

If you are looking for a coffee that has a bit of spice, this is the perfect coffee recipe for you. It has some spice to it which will satisfy any kind of craving you are having.

Makes: 4 Cups

Total Prep Time: 10 Minutes

INGREDIENTS:

- ¾ Cup of Coffee, Ground
- 2 2/3 Cup of Water
- Dash of Cardamom, Ground
- ½ Cup of Milk, Sweetened and Condensed

DIRECTIONS:

1. Using the correct amounts brew up your coffee in the usual way. Once completely brewed, pour your coffee into 4 separate cups.
2. Top each cup with some ground cardamom and at least 2 Tablespoons of your condensed milk. Stir thoroughly to blend everything together perfectly.

Savory Chocolate and Almond Coffee

If you are looking for a coffee drink that can double as a decadent and savory treat, then you have to try this recipe out for yourself. Packed full of chocolate and almond this is the perfect drink to serve alongside your favorite dessert.

Makes: 6 Cups of Coffee

Total Prep Time: 10 Minutes

INGREDIENTS:

- 1/3 Cup of Coffee, Ground
- ¼ tsp. of Nutmeg, Fresh and Ground
- ½ tsp. of Chocolate, Extract Only
- ½ tsp. of Almond, Extract Only
- ¼ Cup of Almonds, Toasted and Chopped Finely

DIRECTIONS:

1. The first thing that you have to do is process your nutmeg and coffee together until you achieve a fine powder.
2. Next add in your extracts and process for an additional 10 seconds longer.
3. Pour your mixture into a bowl and add in your almonds. Stir thoroughly to combine.
4. To brew your coffee, brew as you normally would. Serve while piping hot and enjoy.

Rich and Decadent Chocolate Coffee

This is yet another decadent coffee recipe that you can make and that will leave you craving for more year round. Serve this along a tasty chocolate cake and serve on its own. Either way it is incredibly delicious.

Makes: 6 Cups of Coffee

Total Prep Time: 15 Minutes

INGREDIENTS:

- 2 Tbsp. of Coffee, Instant
- ¼ Cup of Sugar, White
- Dash of Salt, For Extra Taste
- 1 Ounce of Chocolate, Unsweetened and Squared
- 1 Cup of Water
- 3 Cups of Milk, Whole
- Some Whipped Cream

DIRECTIONS:

1. Using a medium sized saucepan, combine your white sugar, water, chocolate squares, coffee and salt together. Place over low heat and stir vigorously or until your chocolate has completely melted.
2. Allow your mixture to simmer for at least 4 minutes, making sure to stir it constantly to prevent burning.
3. Next gradually add in your whole milk, making sure to stir your mixture thoroughly until it is heated again.
4. Once your mixture is piping hot, remove it from heat and beat vigorously using a mixer until your mixture is frothy and foamy.
5. Pour your coffee into coffee cups and serve with a generous helping of whipped cream.

Tasty Mint Chocolate Coffee

If you are a fan of any treat that has a mint chocolate flavor, then I assure you, you will certainly love this kind of coffee. Decadent and packed full of mint flavor, this is one dish that you will want to enjoy over and over again.

Makes:	6 Cups of Coffee
Total Prep Time:	1 Hour and 10 Minutes

INGREDIENTS:

- 1/3 Cup of Coffee, Ground
- 1 tsp. of Chocolate, Extract Only
- ½ tsp. of Mint, Extract Only
- ¼ tsp. of Vanilla Extract

DIRECTIONS:

1. The first thing that you will want to do is place your ground coffee into a blend. The place all of your extract into a measuring cup together. Stir to combine the extracts.
2. Begin to grin your coffee, slowly add in your extract as it blends. Stop the mixing process and make sure to scrap the sides of your blender to get the coffee that sticks to the side of the blend. Continue to process for at least an additional 10 seconds.
3. Store in your refrigerator for at least an hour. Remove and brew as you normally would. Enjoy.

Coconut Flavored Coffee

If you are a huge fan of coconut, then I know you are going to fall in love with this recipe. Packed full of coconut flavor this is going to be one type of coffee that satisfies any coconut lover's cravings.

Makes: 7 Minutes

Total Prep Time: 8 Minutes

INGREDIENTS:

- 2 Cups of Half and Half
- 15 Ounces of Cream of Coconut
- 4 Cups of Coffee, Freshly Brewed and Hot
- Some Whipped Cream, Sweetened

DIRECTIONS:

1. The first thing that you will want to do is bring your half-and-half and coconut cream to a rolling boil in a small sized saucepan over medium heat. Make sure that you stir this cream mixture continuously.
2. Once boiling stir in your coffee. Stir well to combine.
3. Remove from heat and serve into coffee cups. Top with some sweetened whipped cream and enjoy!

EASY ICED COFFEE

This is yet another Iced Coffee recipe that I know avid fans are going to drool over. Very easy to make and incredibly delicious, this recipe can be made by virtually anybody.

Makes: 3 Cups of Iced Coffee

Total Prep Time: 5 Hours and 10 Minutes

INGREDIENTS:

- 2 Cups of Espresso, Freshly Brewed
- ¼ Cup of Sugar, White
- ½ tsp. of Cinnamon, Ground

DIRECTIONS:

1. Using a medium sized saucepan, combine all of your ingredients together and allow all of the ingredients to simmer until completely dissolved.
2. One dissolved, remove your mixture from heat and place inside a metal dish. Cover the dish and place into your freezer and freeze for at least 5 hours.
3. During this time make sure that in 30 minute intervals stir the outer section of your frozen mixture. Continue to freeze until your mixture is firm, but not completely frozen.
4. Before serving make sure that you scrape your mixture by using a fork to lighten it. Enjoy.

Soda and Coffee Surprise

I know that this is a recipe that may not seem like it would be a tasty coffee drink, but trust me it is. It has the smooth flavor that only coffee can offer, but with the fizzle that only soda can offer. I promise you, after trying this recipe once you are going to fall in love with.

Makes:	4 Cups of Coffee
Total Prep Time:	15 Minutes

INGREDIENTS:

- 3 Cups of Coffee, Chilled and Double Strength Variety
- 1 Tbsp. of Sugar, White
- 1 Cup of Half and Half
- 4 Scoops of Ice Cream, Coffee Flavored
- ¾ Cup of Club Soda, Chilled
- Some Whipped Cream, Sweetened
- Some Cherries, Maraschino Variety
- Some Chocolate Curls, For Garnish

DIRECTIONS:

1. The first thing that you will want to do is combine your sugar and coffee together until thoroughly combined.
2. Then gently blend in your half and half and club soda. Blend until evenly mixed. Pour into glasses and make sure that you fill your glass halfway with this mixture.
3. Add in at least 1 scoop of ice cream into each glass. Top off with any remaining soda.
4. Garnish your glass with some whipped cream, chocolate curls and cherries. Serve immediately.

Creamy Coffee Milkshake

There is nothing better than coffee…unless you combine it with ice cream. That is exactly what this recipe is and it is one that you are going to want to make over and over again.

Makes:	5 Cups of Coffee Milkshake
Total Prep Time:	5 Minutes

INGREDIENTS:

- 2 Cups of Milk
- 2 Tbsp. of Sugar, White
- 2 tsp. of Coffee, Instant Variety
- 3 Tbsp. of Ice Cream, Vanilla Flavored
- Some Coffee, Strong and Cold

DIRECTIONS:

1. Add all of your ingredients into a blend. Mix together for at least 5 minutes or until your mix is thoroughly blended.
2. Once blended well pour your mixture into chilled glasses and serve immediately.

Hearty Di Saronno Coffee

What is better than giving your coffee a little pick me up now and then? Now, with this recipe you can do exactly that.

Makes: 2 Cups of Coffee

Total Prep Time: 3 Minutes

INGREDIENTS:

- 1 Ounce of Di Saronno Amaretto
- 8 Ounces of Coffee, Freshly Brewed
- Some Whipped Cream

DIRECTIONS:

1. The first thing that you will want to do is thoroughly mix together your coffee and amaretto together until thoroughly blended.
2. Pour your mixture into a large coffee mug and top off with some whipped cream. Enjoy!

Roman Style Espresso

If you want to enjoy a classic espresso drink that will give you the energy of a Roman soldier, then this is the drink for you. This espresso will give you the energy that your body desperately needs and crave.

Makes:	1 Cup of Coffee
Total Prep Time:	12 Minutes

INGREDIENTS:

- ¼ Cup of Coffee, Finely Ground
- 1 ½ Cup of Water, Cold
- 2 Strips of Lemon, Peel Only

DIRECTIONS:

1. Using a steamed pressure coffee pot, fill up the filter section of it with your water.
2. Place the filter of the pot into its place with your ground coffee. Screw the top and bottom portions of the pot together.
3. Place your coffee pot over medium heat and heat thoroughly until your coffee begins to bubble into the top portion of your pot. Once this happens reduce your heat to low and allow your coffee simmer until it stops bubbling.
4. Remove from heat and serve your coffee immediately. Top off with a lemon peel and enjoy.

THE PERFECT FIRESIDE COFFEE

This is a perfect coffee recipe to use if you ever go camping. It will also help to round out a perfect camping trip nicely, giving you the perfect cup of joe that you deserve.

Makes: 5 Cups of Coffee

Total Prep Time: 7 Minutes

INGREDIENTS:

- 2 Cups of NesQuik
- 2 Cups of Coffee Creamer, Powdered Preferable
- ½ Cup of Sugar, Powdered
- ¾ tsp. of Cinnamon, Ground
- ¾ tsp. of Nutmeg

DIRECTIONS:

1. The first thing that you will want to do is mix all of your ingredients together. Stir together until evenly combined.
2. Then mix at least 4 tsp. of your mixture together with at least 1 cup of water. Let your coffee seep for at least 5 minutes before serving.

Classic Mocha

If you are a fan of classic Mocha from a coffee house, then you are going to want to enjoy this recipe over and over again. This recipe is relatively easy to make and tastes just as good as any coffee house blend.

Makes: 1 Cup of Coffee

Total Prep Time: 5 Minutes

INGREDIENTS:

- ¼ Cup of Creamer, Non Dairy and Powdered
- 1/3 Cup of Sugar, White
- 2 Tbsp. of Cocoa
- ¼ Cup of Coffee, Instant and Dried

DIRECTIONS:

1. Place all of your ingredients into a mixer. Blend on the highest setting until your mixture is well blended.
2. To make one cup of coffee mix together at least 1 ½ tablespoons of your coffee mixture with at least ¾ cup of steaming hot water. Store the rest of your mixture into an air tight container and save for later. Enjoy!

FROZEN CAPPUCCINO

If you are an avid fan of iced coffee, then I know for sure that you are going to love this recipe. It makes a frozen cappuccino that you are going to begging for more.

Makes: 1 Cup of Cappuccino

Total Prep Time: 5 Minutes

INGREDIENTS:

2 Scoops of Yogurt, Vanilla Flavored, Frozen and Evenly Divided
½ Cup of Milk, Whole
1 Tbsp. of Chocolate Mix, Hershey's Brand Preferable
1 ½ tsp. of Coffee, Instant Variety and Granules

DIRECTIONS:

1. The first thing that you will want to do is place at least one scoop of yogurt, chocolate milk mix and coffee into a blender. Blend this mixture for at least 30 seconds or until it is smooth in consistency.
2. Once completely blended, pour your mixture into a tall drinking glass. Top off with some more yogurt and serve at once. Enjoy!

Classic German Coffee

If there is one thing that the Germans know how to do and how to do it right, it is coffee. German coffee is not only smooth as it goes down, but it is also incredibly strong. Take some caution when drinking this drink.

Makes:	5 Cups of Coffee
Total Prep Time:	3 Minutes

INGREDIENTS:

- 5 Cups of Coffee, Strong and Hot
- Some Sugar, White and For Taste
- Some Whipped Cream

DIRECTIONS:

1. Pour your strong coffee into some coffee mugs.
2. Sweeten your coffee with some sugar and stir until the sugar fully dissolves.
3. Top off your coffee with a generous helping of whipped cream and serve immediately.

Traditional Café Au Lait Iced Coffee

Iced coffee is a drink that is steadily growing in popularity with every passing year. This coffee is a very traditional drink that is often made in many Western states. It is incredibly tasty and will soon become a favorite of yours.

Makes: 2 Cups of Iced Coffee

Total Prep Time: 5 Minutes

INGREDIENTS:

- 2 ¼ Cup of Coffee, Freshly Brewed and Cold
- 2 Cups of Milk, Whole
- 2 Cups of Ice, Crushed
- Some Sugar, For Your Taste

DIRECTIONS:

1. You will need to blend all of your ingredients except for your sugar together until thoroughly combined.
2. Next add in as much or as little sugar as you want and continue stirring. Stir until your mixture becomes frothy.
3. Pour into a chilled glass filled with ice and enjoy immediately.

Cinnamon Flavored Iced Coffee

Here is yet another iced coffee recipe that I know you are going to fall in love with. This iced coffee recipe is incredibly rich and surprisingly easy to make. Once you try it for yourself I know that you are going to want to make it over and over again.

Makes: 4 Cups of Iced Coffee

Total Prep Time: 1 Hour and 5 Minutes

INGREDIENTS:

- 4 Cups of Coffee, Strong
- 1 Stick of Cinnamon, Broken Into Small Pieces
- ½ Cup of Cream, Heavy
- Some Coffee Syrup

DIRECTIONS:

1. The first thing that you will want to do is pour your hot coffee over your broken up cinnamon pieces in a medium sized bowl. Cover the bowl and let this mixture sit for at least one hour.
2. After an hour remove the cinnamon and thoroughly stir in your cream.
3. Place this mixture into your fridge and allow to chill.
4. Once your coffee is chilled, pour it into 4 glasses lined with ice and serve immediately.

THE ORIGINAL ICED COFFEE

There are many different recipes for Iced Coffee out there, but none will match this recipe. This is actually the original iced coffee recipe. Trust me, once you get a taste of this coffee you will surely notice the difference.

Makes:	1 Cup of Iced Coffee
Total Prep Time:	5 Minutes

INGREDIENTS:

- ¼ Cup of Coffee, Instant and Regular Blend
- ¼ Cup of Sugar, White
- 1 Cup of Milk, Cold

DIRECTIONS:

1. The first thing that you will want to do is dissolve your instant coffee and sugar together in some hot water.
2. Then stir in your milk and stir to thoroughly combine everything together.
3. Pour this coffee recipe into a glass filled with ice. Feel free to add in some chocolate milk instead of whole milk to give the drink more taste.

SWISS STYLE MOCHA

The Swiss know how to a great tasting cup of coffee, that is for sure. Now you can enjoy a traditional Swiss flavored coffee right from the comfort of your own home.

Makes: 4 Cups of Coffee

Total Prep Time: 5 Minutes

INGREDIENTS:

- ½ Cup of Coffee, Granules and Instant Variety
- ½ Cup of Sugar, White
- 2 Tbsp. of Cocoa
- 1 Cup of Milk, Powder, Nonfat and Dry

DIRECTIONS:

1. You will need to combine all of your ingredients together and make sure that everything is thoroughly mixed. Use at least 1 Tbsp. of your mix to make 1 Cup of coffee. Store the rest of your mix into an airtight container and store for later use.
2. To make your coffee mix in at least 1 Tbsp. of your coffee mix with at least 1 cup of boiling hot water. Stir to thoroughly dissolve your coffee and serve while still piping hot. Enjoy!

Worldwide International Style Coffee

Regardless of what country you are from, where your family originated from or what your ethnic background may be, this coffee recipe is automatically perfect for you. It contains ingredients that are savored all over the world and make this one interesting and great tasting coffee.

Makes: 3 Cups of Coffee

Total Prep Time: 10 Minutes

INGREDIENTS:

- 6 tsp. of Coffee, Instant Variety
- 4 Tbsp. of Cocoa, Unsweetened
- 1 tsp. of Cinnamon, Ground
- 5 Tbsp. of Sugar, White
- Some Whipped Cream

DIRECTIONS:

1. Mix all of your ingredients together except for your whipped cream until thoroughly blended. Set aside.
2. To make your coffee grab a coffee mug and combine at least 1 ½ Cups of boiling hot water with at least 1 tablespoon of your coffee mixture. Stir to thoroughly dissolve your coffee.
3. Top your coffee off with a generous amount of whipped cream. Serve while still hot and enjoy immediately.

Classic Irish Cappuccino

If you are looking for a different cappuccino recipe to enjoy, then you need to try this recipe out for yourself. Packed full of that classic Irish taste that you can't mistake, this is one recipe that you are going to want to make over and over again.

Makes:	2 Cups of Coffee
Total Prep Time:	7 Minutes

INGREDIENTS:

- 3 Ounces of Irish Cream, Bailey's Brand
- 5 Ounces of Coffee, Hot
- Some Dessert Topping, Pressurized
- Dash of Nutmeg, Ground

DIRECTIONS:

1. The first thing that you will want to do is pour your Irish cream into a medium to large sized coffee mug. Then fill it up with some hot black coffee.
2. Top your mug with at least a single layer of dessert topping. Finish off by garnishing with a sprinkle of ground nutmeg. Serve while piping hot and enjoy immediately.

Italian Style Coffee with Chocolate

Italian Coffee is also a nice change, especially if you are used to Dunkin Donuts or Starbucks on a daily basis. This coffee is incredibly smooth, yet packed full of flavor that you will immediately enjoy.

Makes: 4 Cups of Coffee

Total Prep Time: 7 Minutes

INGREDIENTS:

- 2 Cups of Coffee, Hot and Strong
- 2 Cups of Cocoa, Hot and Traditional Variety
- Some Whipped Cream
- Orange Peel, Finely Grated

DIRECTIONS:

1. The first thing that you will want to do is combine at least ½ cup of your hot coffee and ½ cup of hot cocoa into 4 separate mugs.
2. Top your mugs off with a generous helping of whipped cream and sprinkle with orange peel for garnish. Serve immediately.

Italian Style Mocha Espresso

This is yet another Italian Style coffee recipe that I know you are certainly going to enjoy. It makes an espresso that is incredibly smooth, yet packed full of caffeine, giving you the energy that you desperately need to greet the day ahead.

Makes: 7 Cups of Coffee

Total Prep Time: 10 Minutes

INGREDIENTS:

- 1 Cup of Coffee, Instant Variety
- 1 Cup of Sugar, White
- 4 ½ Cups of Milk, Non Fat and Dry
- ½ Cup of Cocoa

DIRECTIONS:

1. Stir all of your ingredients in a small sized bowl until thoroughly combined. Pour into a blender and blend until completely processed.
2. Then add 2 tablespoons of your coffee mixture into a coffee mug with at least 1 cup of hot water. Stir until coffee fully dissolves. Serve immediately and enjoy.

Maple Flavored Coffee

This is one coffee recipe that is one of my personal favorites. This coffee is great when paired with a breakfast filled with fluffy pancakes and hearty bacon. It is semi-sweet to taste and will certainly leave you and your family drooling for more.

Makes: 4 Cups of Coffee

Total Prep Time: 8 Minutes

INGREDIENTS:

- 1 Cup of Half and Half
- ¼ Cup of Maple Syrup, Your Favorite Kind
- 1 Cup of Coffee, Hot and Freshly Brewed
- Some Whipped Cream, Sweetened

DIRECTIONS:

1. The first thing that you will have to do is heat up your half and half and maple syrup together in a medium sized saucepan. Heat up over medium heat, making sure to stir your mixture constantly until your mixture is completely heated through.
2. Next stir in your coffee and continue to stir until your coffee completely dissolves.
3. Serve your coffee into medium to large sized coffee mugs and top with a generous amount of sweetened whipped cream and enjoy.

Conclusion

There are so many coffee recipes out that that I know it can be difficult to choose which one you like the most. Hopefully through the use of this book that decision can be made much easier for you. Each coffee listed within this book has its own unique taste and unique flavor, giving all the coffee lovers out there a wide variety of options to choose from. Choose carefully as every sip that you have will change your opinions of which types of coffee you like the most.

Coffee is a great way to rejuvenate your body with the energy it needs to survive throughout the day while giving you all of the benefits that it has to offer. Hopefully this book will help raise your spirits and help you to find different flavors of coffee that you will eventually fall in love.

19594212R00068

Printed in Great Britain
by Amazon